You are, your cure.

Cristina Firtala

You are, your cure.

I want to dedicate this book, to all the people who reached what they thought was rock bottom. To all the people who thought they couldn't survive their battles. This book exists to remind you that, you are your cure. You will overcome every battle that you will face.

You are, your cure.

Introduction

From the production of "As Long As You're Breathing" a poetry collection centred around how we express the depths of our human experience, be it love, loss or any structure of pain, I present to you...

"You are, your cure" an extension of our expressed experiences, but this time, this poetry collection defines our way out, through self-healing and the realisation that you and I, are our cure. We can heal ourselves, and we can do it together. Separate pathways, two roads, two self-healing journeys and one book. I hope this poetry collection helps you, but most importantly, I hope it reminds you that you are the centre of your world, and the most powerful centre that you will ever meet.

You are, your cure.

The life that ended.

Our entire existence is not measured by,

the love we gave,
the success we gained
or,
the assets that we obtained,

but by the circumference of everything we wanted to but
could not do.

Could not be.

You are, your cure.

How?

How do you tell the world that fire doesn't burn enough,
anymore?

How do you tell love that you no longer treasure it with the
same intensity, anymore?

How do you tell yourself that you did everything, but it
wasn't enough, anymore?

You breathe.

This is the one and only life that you will ever own.

Breathe.
Accept.
Process.

And then process again, a little bit more.

Reincarnate the pain into something beautiful.

Release.

And step forward, no matter how hard the pain drags you
backwards.

There isn't enough time in this life- to let pain consume you.

You are, your cure.

You are, your cure.

A ripened heart

Dear depression,

Do not swallow me yet,
I have still, a few more days until my expiration date,

wait a little bit longer,

let me sweeten, just a little bit more...

By reading in coffee shops on rainy days,
travelling the world in the hot summer rays,
discovering pain, joy & love that will solve my heart's
maze,

dear depression,

do not swallow me yet,

I promise that if you give me a few more days,
you will find me too ripe, too sweet for your selective
taste,
for now, I am bitter,
but I yearn to let time ripen me,
into a fruit that is yet to be discovered.

You are, your cure.

One bursting with the most unforgettable flavours, of this entire lifetime.

You are, your cure.

Two types of love

We communicate through wind,
through meeting eyes between the beautiful grey and
exquisite brown,
you are gold and I am silver.
You are the sun and I - the moon.
You are autumn and I am winter.
Your love glows with heat, and mine protects with ice.

You are, your cure.

To the worst days of your life.

I cannot say that life offers more,

because it doesn't.

You just have to learn to take more.

To breathe more, to feel more, to experience more.

We are either futile beings in an abandoned universe of coincidental miracles,

or,

we are fated by a series of planned occurrences with precision.

Whilst both exist as parallel universes,

imagine them not as separate, but whole,

two segments of one universe.

So, what if our lives, are simply, one fated coincidence?

You are, your cure.

Smiles?

I cannot remember the way I used to smile.

Before, smiling was a protection from reality,

before, smiling was a rejection from fatality,

before, smiling was the projection of sanity.

The only thing I remember, was that life was not supposed to feel so heavy, so blurred, so fragmented.

It was supposed to be at least some, smiles.

Smiles that were actually happiness.

You are, your cure.

Framed for stolen time.

To be young was once known to be freedom, adventure and discovery,

yet somehow now it is futility, emotional lethargy and tragedy.

I cannot name love as the culprit,

nor generational progression as a suspect,

or time as the victim.

But I can name you, as the person of interest.

Because you are in control of your life.

You are, your cure.

To play, to live.

We play all the games of suffering,

juggling anxiety with a timer,

three, overthinking,

two, catastrophic thoughts.

And one, overwhelmed, the balls drop.

Are you going to pick them up?

Bowling, with pins of depression,
except, that the alley pinsetters no longer work,
the arcade is an abandoned building,
waiting for your depression to restore,
so that you can restore the arcade of, your future.

Aligning your cue stick at the most precise angle,
but you get pushed, so the pool game of your compulsive
thoughts begin, the ball rolls and rolls, and your
thoughts
repeat and repeat, until you lose and accept mental
defeat.

Do you replay, or do you delay?

We play all the games of suffering, but the difference is,
when we play suffering's games, we do not play to win.

You are, your cure.

We play to distract our soul from a world where happiness is self-destructive, and pain is reliable.

So, I guess we have to play, because if we don't, we feel nor joy, or pain, we become paralysed.

You are, your cure.

Guilty, or pleading regret?

I sometimes find myself confused between guilt and regret.

To feel like I have shrivelled up into a single molecule of existence,

because I feel that I deserve nothing more.

Or,

to want to break free from this molecular confinement and find a way to revitalise my existence, for the sole purpose of fixing everything.

The reason that I am confused, is because guilt swallows you like quicksand,

but regret- regret is a tornado that forces you to make things right.

So, where do I exist in the midst of choosing, with freedom laced in the molecules that

I have become.

You are, your cure.

You are, your cure.

A secret.

Suffering is not a part of being human,

it is the key ingredient, the most important piece, the component that allows us to

exist.

It swims through our bloodstream.

It flutters through our oxygen.

It grows with our bones.

But we do everything in our power to erase, to minimise our existence,

suffering.

But what if I told you a secret?

Your suffering is the only thing you can hold power over.

Not love, not joy not thrill or excitement,

Suffering.

Because you are formulated from molecules of pain, particles of agony.

You can remould every part of you that suffers, into artwork.

You are, your cure.

You are, your cure.

Love me where?

I am uncertain as to whether love can swim, float or drown.

I am only certain, that love can walk on land.

So, maybe this is the problem.

We force love to exist in the habitats of hearts that, only crave the ocean.

You are, your cure.

What love says

His power was not making her smile,

not laugh or feel joy.

His power was silencing her.

He knew, and only he knew, how to freeze the
hurricanes of her anxiety.

How to perform magic tricks to make her believe that
her thoughts can be spilt,

half to her, half to him.

How to dance with her, in ways that words do not know
how to bounce or twirl.

His power remained here, in ways that silenced her pain,

to let her hear joy's side of the story.

Loss.

This is where it all begins.

Once upon a time something strange, unusual showed
up at a young child's door.

The child, by the name of Life, knew nothing of Loss, but
made it feel at home, welcomed it in.

But when it was time for Loss to go home,
Loss took the child's dummy.
The child screamed, kicked and fought for it.
But it was gone.

A few years later, the child hardly remembered the
dummy.
But the child found out that their mum was sick,
the child didn't understand the severity,
the depth that this sickness had pierced through her.
Later that same year, Loss came by. Loss tapped the
child's shoulder to comfort them.
But she passed and Loss disappeared.

Skipping a few decades, the child was no longer young,
they became an adult.

You are, your cure.

They are now settled into the job of their dreams, they haven't forgotten about their mother or gotten over the pain, but this time they learnt to cope, learnt to co-exist with Loss in their life.

It sounds so easy, just accept.

But we do not want to forgive loss, because we think accepting is forgetting, moving on with life and being okay.

This isn't acceptance.

Acceptance is forgiving loss, but learning how to show who you lost, that they can see life through you now, so show whoever you lost the best parts of life.

Co-exist with loss.

You are, your cure.

We are all born rich.

Not the type that makes your pockets itch,
I am talking about emotional wealth,
we are born into emotional health,
and if you forget that,
withdraw a second from your life's cash point,
and spend that second realising that you exist as the
world's most intricate being,
emotional freedom, don't watch it fleeting.
You are capable of healing shattering hearts,
reconstructing self-esteem, motivating the exhausted,
and revitalising even the death of any soul,
because you are born into emotional wealth.
Capable of ruling your world with only your heart and
mind, lips to rewind,
the words that you struggle to find.
You may or may not have what you desire right now,
but what I can guarantee that you own, is your
emotional power,
so, seize it, learn to control it and use it as your most
fierce weapon.

You are, your cure.

You want my advice?

Stop thinking, questioning and feeling, needing,
pleading for too much.
Anything in excess is toxic.
Anything in excess is chaotic.
To think too much is like smoke with no fire.
Walking up an endless hill, higher and higher,
to question too much, it's an attempt to breathe faster
and faster per second.

You are tiring yourself out pointlessly,

needlessly and ceaselessly.

To need too much.
To want too much.
To have too much,

is to not really have anything at all.

You are, your cure.

To be unfair is to live fair.

I grew up being told to play fair.
Games, exams, behaviour.
To play fair and be fair.
But nothing in the existence of this life is fair.
Maybe it was our parents' responsibility to relieve the
pain by incorporating some sort of fairness to an unjust
world.
But fairness is an unobtainable euphoric concept,
from sickness, to discrimination, prejudice, racism,
sexism, poverty, imprisonment to loss to death, I could
go on forever.
My point is, to play fair I need to do three things,

Be selfless
Be free of greed
And increase my compassion

The problem lies not in the obtainment of these things,
but in the maintenance.
We all start fair, but somewhere along the game we
become corrupt because if we see our opponent
cheating,
we think, so why should I play fair?

And the answer is, you shouldn't.

You are, your cure.

Always manipulate the systems and the mechanisms you
hold, to benefit you,
but here's the difference, not just to benefit you.

So maybe we cannot play fair, but if you cheat, you must
cheat your way to help not yourself, but both you and
your opponent.

If you must break the rules, break to heal.

You are, your cure.

Heartache.

I do not feel the crumbles of heartache,
playing hide and seek in the cracks of every new
template,

but I do feel, the entire, whole existence of it, crumbling
all over my face.
Into my eyes they go, blinding me? No.

Just altering my vision.

Into my mouth? Yes.

Feeding me the things that cause me an intolerance,

to lactose? No.

To every crumb you let fall upon my lifetime,

this is heartache, confusion.

crumbles of pain you can't seem to clean entirely,

until you change the bedsheets, hoover the carpet and
clean every particle of doubtful and reluctant dust, from
the home of your heart.

You are, your cure.

You are, your cure.

Mood swings or trauma?

I am treading on fire, bare feet on flames,
except I am walking on a heat proof mat.
But it feels like fire, so I say it is fire.
I am breathing in steam, coughing, I am suffocating.

Though I am breathing in the steam from my cooker,
but it feels like so much, so I assume that it is too much.

I cannot separate the intensity from reality when they
co-exist as soulmates.
To feel flames on my skin, but know the floor is
moderately heated.
So, I let both fight. War?
Not really.
A simple rock, paper, scissors.

And if by some magical chance intensity wins, tell reality
that we can all work together.

To let reality dim irritability,

so, irritability lives intensely, in reality.

You are, your cure.

Who are you?

You will love this entire world before you love yourself.

You'll love travelling because it brings you excitement?

You'll love this person because they are so sweet.

And you'll love millions of things because they give you
so much?

But you're the combination of everything you'll ever
learn to love,

so why don't you make it easier for yourself, and instead
of running to find everything in everyone,

love who you are, and everything you're looking for, will
be everything you have found.

You are, your cure.

One

Don't let anything in this entire lifetime consume you completely.

You have one mind, one soul and one lifetime.

So let love in, welcome it with open arms, but let it accommodate with luxurious decor and let it decorate that chamber with jewels, silk bedding and anything it wants, but only into one chamber of your heart.

Accept pain, don't refrain, but let it sit on the floor of an empty chamber, one chamber only.

And allow success to reign the chamber, to put up its posters and certificates, but only in that one room of your heart, one chamber.

Never allow anyone to occupy every room because the second you do, that love or success steps on a tendon too hard, pushed against a capillary too hard- your entire heart weakens, and you have no control.

And life is too short for that,

too short to let anything destroy you completely.

You are, your cure.

Perspective

Being able to evaluate the most distinctive and
indistinguishable fibres of what make us selective
humans is everything.
From intellectual power to literary supremacy.
Nothing matters.
Power to see ourselves as everything.
Control over our emotions.
Time as our assistant.
Intensity as our freedom.
Awareness as our anchor.

You are, your cure.

Figuring it out?

Forget the artificial or superficial love of another soul

Forget the

And the

And the

The only way through, that will guarantee you stability
and reliability,

 is to condition yourself to believe that you are the
powerhouse of your life,

that you are complete and everything you need lays in
front of you.

You are in pain?

Tell yourself the words that you'd tell your soulmate.

You are struggling?

Motivate yourself the way you wish you could?

You are, your cure.

The only way is to let yourself feel it- control.

Then tell yourself that everything is temporary, and you will move on and face the next challenge.

 Because you don't have the choice to sit around and cry forever.

We are all born through the same door to death,

none of the sadness or pain will save you,

you may as-well pretend to be happy until you don't recognise sadness by its name, how it looks or the feeling.

And then you will learn to never let anything unfamiliar,

anything dangerous into your life.

You are, your cure.

Knock Knock.

"Hello, open the door, let me in?"

"Can you hear me, hello, open the door it's cold."

But the door never opened.

Empty and shaking.

I can only apologise for the doors you stood in front of
begging to open,

love, luck, healing, success,

that never opened for you not even when you were
begging, screaming or hysterical.

Because this is the way the world works,

its fuel runs on exposure that becomes perspective,
heartbreak, failure or trauma.

You are, your cure.

Its hydration runs on the liquid we let pour from our eyes destroying our vision for a

split second,

while the world recuperates but we are okay by then.

Its emotion runs on whatever we drop, irreplaceable moments of love or pain,

it soaks it up and we never get it back,

a sponge that becomes so overwhelmed that it blocks the entrances,

of every entrance in the house of love,

every front door of success and every entrance that we beg to open.

It can't because we are human.

But this is the thing.

This is it.

We beg for doors to open that are blocked because they are so filled with everything

we already have,

but refuse to love.

You are, your cure.

You are, your cure.

Tell me more.

So, is there more?
After death.
Is there purpose,
is there meaning behind our eyes,
is this oxygen going to free us,
or is it the end?

The end.

Our existence is fuelled by questions.

We all ask ourselves if there is too much sugar in that
drink.

If we spent too long trying to think.
If we will miss the goal if we blink.
If it's a girl or boy, blue or pink.

Because we know the answer range, but never the
correct stage.

Too much, we know it's a yes, or no?

Is there more after death... possibly or possibly not?

You are, your cure.

We will always be so close to yes or no,

yet thousands of miles away from ever knowing if it's yes
or no.

What I am trying to say is that questions explain our
knowledge,

but they also send us on voyages,

and this specific one will send you into the voyage of lost
time.

You are, your cure.

Being human.

I think you have forgotten,

that you are not an engineered design,

an electrical software programmed to complete
everything with only perfection.

You are only human.

You are not programmed to feel happy all the time, okay
or competent.

You are allowed to make mistakes, to fail, to mess up, to
get things wrong.

You are only a human being.

Do you understand that being alive just means existing,

it's just breathing, experiencing, it is just being,

you have no expectation to live as if you are a robot.

Don't try to get rid of the humanity, the flaws, the
mistakes.

You are, your cure.

Use your humanity to your advantage,

because if there is anything in this entire lifetime that
you can master better than anything, it is being human.

You are, your cure.

A cure only the past can offer.

Do you know what the worst thing about life is?
It's not loss, nor pain, or discomfort.
It's the reality of realisation.
The abundance of realisation.
The lack, the overflow, the too little crumbs.

It is the saddest thing because when there is a lack of
realisation now, there is an overflow later.

And no matter how hard you convince the present you
that one day there will be too much, so much realisation,
that if you don't change now, it's pointless, you can't.

Because it speaks a language that only your future soul
can understand,

a language underdeveloped now, tethered to your soul
and for as long as you live you will learn that language
fluently day by day, until you are fluent, but you cannot
speak.

And you just have to learn to live with an exceptional
proficiency in the art of language, that you can no longer
speak.

You are, your cure.

That's why realisation is truly, the saddest.

Because the cure to realisation's pain, is the past, and that's truly the one cure we will never obtain.

You are, your cure.

We want guarantees, don't we?

We want solidity, prosperous certainty, security, don't we?

Well, here is something that is quite almost guaranteed.

One day you will find yourself struggling, in pain, filled with hot knots of anger- set on fire.

Days where time feels like solitary confinement.

Tears that won't stop pouring like a storm,

or curled up, suffering.

And the guarantee is that you will find yourself asking *how am I supposed to get through this?*

That is where the guarantee, certainty, solidity and anything that physically assures you security- lives.

Because the next few days after,

you find yourself in a constant loop of swimming, floating and drowning.

You are, your cure.

Loop after loop because you learn that this is healing.

And no one teaches you these things,

but it's good that they are built in survival roots that we
all have,

we all carry with us, until some of them fall out and we
become exposed,

our pain to the world ... and suddenly we are the bad
guys.

But maybe, we need to learn how to share our survival
tools with the world,

and then maybe, when our hammer of anger falls, we
won't be so aggressive, maybe when our saws of panic
fall, we won't cause so much damage and maybe when
the crowbar of depression falls, we won't be so shocked.

That is not a guarantee, we like guarantee, we love
solidity, prosperity, anything that we are promised,

but maybe when we learn how to allow our mental
health to breathe freely,

we can begin to create a world that loves freedom and
isn't so scared of the unknown.

You are, your cure.

Some of us live lives encompassed by crimes.

No, I don't mean just physical.

I'm talking about emotional, psychological and
intellectual crimes.

Some of us are serving a life's sentence convicted by the
judge of guilt.

A mind protected by the prison guards of hatred.

A soul surrounded by convicts of self-hatred,

inmates of self-destruction because that is easier, locking
up our trauma is easier than
facing the trial,

the emotional paperwork, the time and the energy,

that is easier, than pleading innocent to the crimes that
you didn't commit.

There is no evidence that you are guilty for what you
wish you had done, the mistakes you made and the love
you forgot to give,

You are, your cure.

other than your statement.

So, change it, you only have one life.

Don't spend it self-imprisoned by your pain.

Because you are stronger.

Realise this.

You are your own emotional solicitor.

Your own psychological evaluator.

And your own logical judge.

Whatever your mind fools you to think,

believe that you are stronger, and you gain power in the court of life.

You are, your cure.

Measuring pain.

I sat here, in my room, anywhere really.

Wondering why it won't go away,

the feeling of the stones of your pain turning into bricks,
into boulders that you can no longer push away.

I wonder, sitting here,

if love really heals us,

or if it's the love we give ourselves that does that fixing,

but I learn, day by day?

That when your stones of pain turn into bricks,

they are not growing to increase your suffering,

but they grow in order to give you the ability to build a
home, brick by brick.

You build with the pain.

I learn day by day,

You are, your cure.

That the bricks turning into boulders not only give you a solid foundation but serve as monuments of your soul's strength.

I learn day by day,

that healing is pain, growing in order to serve a higher purpose.

To surface.

So, the pain can heal.

I sit here wondering, when everything will end.

But I look around, and the pain has become pebbles again.

I can brush them away.

I learn, day by day?

That healing will be okay.

But it never goes, until it grows into boulders,

into pebbles.

You are, your cure.

Into nothing at all.

You are, your cure.

Caution- the floor is slippery.

You need to find one thing you love, with passion,
and dedicate three quarters of your heart to it,
only three quarters.
Because if by some tragic chance- it ends, breaks or
leaves you,
you need to have a quarter of your untouched heart to
fall on.
To help you, to be there for you.

You are, your cure.

Trauma.

You follow me into a cage.
Turn the timer on my anger and lock me shut.
You film me,
screaming, kicking, fighting.
Laughing, smiling, crying.
Fighting again. And again. And again.
You say cut.
Let me out.
Set me free.
Free from an entrapment that sprinkles glittered words
into my head.

You are, your cure.

Stay centred.

Love in all magnitudes, is the centre of every dimension.

To do the things you love.

To feel the things, you love.

To spend time with those you love.

Love is not all, but it is the centre of every dimension,

be it joy or pain,

 it exists at the core of every moment.

You are, your cure.

A trick?

No, a misunderstanding.

Some of us don't get to say it's okay,
tomorrow we will feel better,

Because for some of us,
grief will still wake up with us.
Anxiety will still linger.
Depression will still weigh us down.

That,

is like saying...

It is okay to drown today, as long as we decide to swim
tomorrow.

Because if you let yourself drown today, tomorrow you will be coughing up water, instead of learning how to swim better.

Be very careful with how comfortable you let pain accommodate in your soul.

You are, your cure.

You are, your cure.

Here it is, the truth.

No matter how many times you call the firefighters,
no matter how many times they extinguish your fire, as
long as you have fuel and oxygen,

it can start again.

No matter how many times you take that medication,
how many times you go to therapy.

As long as you are alive, pain can still ignite again.

The hard reality is that we cannot extinguish pain from
the world.

No matter what you do, you will feel loss, anger? Hate?
Betrayal?

Suffering.

Because the combination of fuel and oxygen is fire.

The combination of life and our existence is pain.

So, learn not how to extinguish fire,

You are, your cure.

but learn how to manage, to control the flames.

You are, your cure.

Beautiful

I know, trust me, I know,

that life is full of pain,

heavy,

heavy pain.

But there are things so beautiful,

so powerful,

that they consume you,

completely unaware.

Like your first love,
souls that dance across the sky above,

or your last goodbye,
a beautiful word that no amount of joy can erase.

Our firsts are known to be like magic,

and our lasts so beautifully tragic.

But what about the middle?

The in-between,
The rest of our life.

You are, your cure.

The centre is always the best part.

The centre of a cake,

or pie,

I know they say save the best till last,

but I think it's time to change that,

save the best till now.

Turn your life, the centre, into something even more
extraordinary than the first,

and,

even more powerful than the last.

You are, your cure.

You will be okay, I promise.

"Okay?

Are you kidding me?"

Please do not forget.

That grief does not just disapear.

The pain does not just vanish.

You just learn how to live with pain as your companion.

Stop wasting your energy trying to find a cure to the pain,

because you are, your cure.

You will be okay, I promise.

"Okay."

You are, your cure.

Cherish your life.

You don't get more than the beautiful love that you
have,
you don't get another chance to feel it's glow,
do not waste a single second hurting that love,
because regret is not just a feeling,
it is an illness, one that is so hard, so incredibly hard to
cure.

Save yourself the pain, and treasure real love -with every
ounce of your being.

You are, your cure.

"What is the saddest word in the dictionary?"

Almost...

But in the end, it doesn't matter.

It doesn't matter if you didn't quite make it.

It doesn't matter if your heart broke along the way.

Or if your dreams fell from your pocket on your way home.

Just like it doesn't matter if you did quite make it,

if you healed from that broken heart.

And if you went back to pick up your dreams.

Because in the end, it doesn't matter.

Things don't go to plan.

People lose people.

And suffering is quite literally our DNA.

Live while you can.

You are, your cure.

Live with a heart full of love.

Live with a mind that's gasping for adventure.

Live with a soul that dances with only wholehearted
twirls and turns.

Because in the end it doesn't matter what you did or did
not do.

Your world will end someday, and it will just be you,

so, make it a world that only dreams could conquer.

A world where the magic of humanity is true.

You are, your cure.

Vintage love

We search in vintage stores,
for unique pieces that only our love can restore,
we bid on antiques like the ceramic will enrich our
homes,
and we treasure the classics because they freeze time.
What I am trying to say to you,

is that difference, is beauty.

Just like you find old vintage clothes beautiful, because
they are different, unique,

you should find the differences between people,
beautiful and unique.

We are all exclusive versions of humanity, with
differences so vast, so powerful, that if your love was to
touch them with kindness, the world could be so
beautiful.

Because difference is what makes the world so beautiful.

You are, your cure.

Finding your heart.

We watched the sun rise, into your brown eyes,
and we watched the sun go down, with your smile,
an upside-down frown,
then we watched the years go by,
words of honey, sour conversations, torn up dedications,
glued back together, soft fingerprints, caresses made of
feathers,
and heavy hands, boulders of disagreements.

Until I watched the sun rise, without your brown eyes.

And I watched the sun go down, with my smile, an
upside-down frown.

We lived through love because that was the whole point,

and now we live through life, except that love is no
longer what we live on, oxygen is.

This happens and it's okay.

Don't let a lost love, deprive you of a newly found life.

You are, your cure.

The only way out.

If you don't live through the trauma, you live inside it.

You are, your cure.

Grief

You walk across every street, of every town.

Pleading for help, screaming in defeat.

Because you have lost everything that was once so
sweet.

Sugar is now an artificial sweetener.

Sour is no longer lemon zest, but gummies filled with
a sour test.

To test you for anything that is real.

Because denial is the crown you steal,

wearing it like the world is your empire.

You are, your cure.

Nothing will last.

I want to tell you something that could change your entire life.

Something that will make all the pain dissolve.
Something that would make everything okay.

So that the pain you feel won't keep slicing your joy,

or the broken parts of you that are shattered.

When you step forward towards happiness and the shards dig in.

You breathe and the shards dig in.

You fight and the broken glass of your entire existence cuts you.
Slices, slashes, all of you.

Glass everywhere.

Pain everywhere.

But I can tell you something that will sweep up all the glass and detain the weapon that slices your joy.

And that's that nothing will last.

You are, your cure.

The pain, it will dissolve.

The happiness, it will pass.

The discomfort, it will change.

You are bound to life by a simple sentence keeping you hostage, nothing lasts.

Now.

You can make yourself at home in that sentence, or you can fight to try and escape.

But I just wanted to warn you, if you fight the reality that nothing lasts, you will miss every infinity of joy that you would have held in the palm of your hands, no I didn't say keep, but hold, if you surrendered to life.

When I say surrender it doesn't mean you give up,

it means you find peace; it means you make a home in whatever this life is.

Nothing lasts.

You are, your cure.

Surviving.

It all comes down to the first thing you think about
when you open your eyes.

The choice is there.

And there are two.

You can either drown in the pain,

or pick yourself up.

And sometimes you need to put your head
underwater, but if you do,
do it in the shallow end so that when you stand back
up it's easy for you to breathe again.

And other times you will swim laps into the deep
end,

but most importantly,

you need to remember that if you learn to swim it
doesn't mean you won't be affected by the wind
waves and tides,

it just means that you're prepared to face it.

Because that's all life is about, it's learning how to go
through the worst possible pain and make it out

You are, your cure.

alive.

It's surviving every ocean storm, and teaching your future self that pain is not an obstacle, that pain shows us power.

You are, your cure.

Your world.

There's just one thing you need to remember,

and that's that the universe does not end, when your world does.

Take this as you will,

but there is so much comfort in those words,

that if the worst thing has happened to you,

it's not the end,

the best thing will also happen to you.

The universe does not end when your world does.

That even if you can't figure out what the purpose of being here is,

the opportunities to find out are endless.

The universe does not end when your world does.

You are, your cure.

That if you are numb from the pain,

remind yourself the anaesthetic will wear off.

The universe does not end when your world does.

Everything is temporary.

Everything is momentary.

Because at the end of your world, after the chaos, the fight, and struggle.

The only thing that matters is knowing that you tried to capture everything you dreamed of.

That's all that matters.

You are, your cure.

How to heal.

There is no such thing as the right or wrong way to
heal.

Healing,

if it was ever possible to compare to anything,

would be compared to mountain climbing.

In your heart you want to get to the top of the
mountain to see the world from a

different perspective,

but sometimes your leg slips off,

and that's okay.

Because you need to always remember you have a
harness attached,

you are safe.

One step back does not mean one step back to the
start.

You are, your cure.

It means you are learning how to climb better,

you are learning what you would do,

if that was to ever happen again.

The best thing about healing is that as long as you
want to get better,

there is nothing in this world that can stop you,

because you are, your cure.

You are, your cure.

Control

If you woke up this morning feeling like nothing is worth it anymore,

or feeling like you don't see a point in the life you're living.

I'm going to give you one simple tip that I hope will change that.

If you don't feel happy with the life you have, find something within that life to be happy about.

You see the thing is, we would run miles to find something that makes us smile.

We would climb mountains to see something beautiful.

But what we are not doing is looking inside our own life and finding something to feel grateful about.

At the end of the day it's simple.

Life is hard and so painful.

You can either live making it beautiful,

or you live that way forever.

You are, your cure.

You are in control of the way you handle your pain.

You are, your cure.

Anxiety

Almost every moment is spent in anxiety's palm.
What if this doesn't go to plan?
What if we don't make it?
What if we lose everything?
And I know you're probably expecting me to reassure
you, to tell you that all the what ifs won't happen,
but I know anxiety far too well to know, that won't help
you.
What I will say, is this,
what if all the what ifs did happen?
If you didn't make it to your dream,
if things didn't go to plan,
and if you did lose everything,
you will still be okay.
You will survive anything.

You are, your cure.

The difference between.

The difference between the life of a person who doesn't
believe in happiness and the life of a person who does, is
not the end result.
Nothing can save you from the inevitable death.
The difference is, one lives a beautiful life,
and one lives a difficult one.

You are, your cure.

Open soul.

The best advice I can give you,
is most probably this,
open your mind at all times, to all dimensions and to all
the impossible and possible options,
because you are limited to human capacity, you cannot
possibly know the crazy realities that exist out there,
so, keep your mind open, no matter how heavy the door
is.

You are, your cure.

Inside out

As hard as this is to believe,
There is better, than the best thing that ever happened
to you, if it is also, the most painful thing that has ever
happened to you.

You are, your cure.

One moment

Things will go wrong.
People will leave.
Time will hurt you.
And life will not be fair to you.

But apart from all of that,

things will also go right, when they will.
People will stay when they love you.
Time will also heal you.
And life will be fair in unfair ways.

So apart from all the bad or the good,
the reason that it's worth living,
is because like fireworks, the good parts are short
lived, but it doesn't stop you from watching them, it
doesn't stop the fireworks themselves from
illuminating the entire sky, even if it's just for a
moment.
Because that's all life is.
One moment,
an epic moment.

You are, your cure.

Captive and free

Let me tell you the truth,
the sour, bitter and salty truth.

Choosing not to sugar coat my words.

It does not matter whether you live on your dream
island,
whether you have everything you ever wanted,
whether you achieved your biggest goal.

If your mind is not free, you will never be.

Because it doesn't matter whether your body is
sleeping in the world's most beautiful palace, if your
mind is still an abandoned building.

Always renovate and refurbish your most important
home first, before you choose to spend your life
chasing any external happiness.

To keep it short,

treat your mind like the powerhouse that runs your
body, your home.

You are, your cure.

Food

I bet you've heard the phrase "food is not your
enemy" about a thousand times.

But when your mind becomes a glacier at the thought
of gaining weight?

Losing weight,
stabilising weight,
food isn't exactly your companion.

But I want to describe food to you in a different way,

when you were little,

and your favourite toy was running out of battery,
you probably did everything in your power to find
new batteries, so that it worked at its full potential.

Nothing's changed.

When you use your phone now and it's running on
low charge it still works,
but you do everything you can to find a charger,
because you want it to work to its full potential right?

And when you need to go to work, or school,
you may not have eaten yet,
so why don't you do everything you can to find food?

Because yes, without lunch you will still live.

You are, your cure.

 Yes,

without breakfast you will still live,

and yes, without dinner you will still live,

but you won't be functioning to your full potential.

Food is not designed to fill in your appearance like teddy bear stuffing.

It is designed to fuel your life.

So that you can function to your full potential.

You are, your cure.

What is the key?

The key is finding something,
anything,
that does these two things concurrently.

Something that brings you comfort and benefits you
at the same time.

You are, your cure.

Lessons

I think one of the most important things I have learnt
as an adult,
is that I don't know everything.
And I will never be too wise to learn more,
because I will simply never know everything.
This is why, keeping an open mind, at all times is the
biggest lesson to learn.
In all situations, even those that seem impossible,
keep an open mind.
Because that is the power, in being human.

You are, your cure.

Don't rush,

Sorry, where are my manners?
Please, don't rush.
Everything you can't wait for, will happen.
Everything you dream of will come.
But right now,
your life right now,
be it good or bad,
will never come again.
This is the only time you'll ever be able to live this
present life.

You are, your cure.

Satisfaction

Did you know that even if you're craziest dream came true,

that even if you achieved everything you always wanted,

there would still be something you would complain about.

Whether it's the million-pound house being too modern or too rustic,

or whether it's that one awkward green wall in in your studio apartment,

you will always find something to complain about,

something you don't love don't enjoy can't stand don't understand.

Can't seem to get your head around,

you will always find something to complain about.

That's it.

Happiness isn't something you dream of achieving someday.

It's something you work on today and every single day.

You are, your cure.

Don't listen.

Don't listen to the people who tell you that you are
too old to heal your inner child.
Life is way too short to not indulge in your childhood
dreams.

You are, your cure.

My conclusion.

After all this writing, all the poetry that my heart and mind can design,

I still don't have the answer to everything, I still don't have every single thing figured out.

And that's okay.

We don't need to have the whole world figured out,
time is just a train ride,
or rather, a tourist attraction.

A train tour, and just like you don't rush the tourist train to the destination only, you enjoy every sight, every stop, every view along the way, that is time.

There would really be no point of the tourist tour train, if it didn't stop at every sight along the way.

That is life, and we will figure out every little detail as we go.

And I promise, everything will be okay,

but for now,

Enjoy this present moment, because even if the present isn't exactly where you want to be, there is something in this present that you will never experience again.

You are, your cure.

Make the most of it, of everything.

You are, your cure.

You are your cure.

You are, your cure.

Have you read Cristina Firtala's other books?

You are, your cure.

As Long As You're Breathing

Cristina Firtala

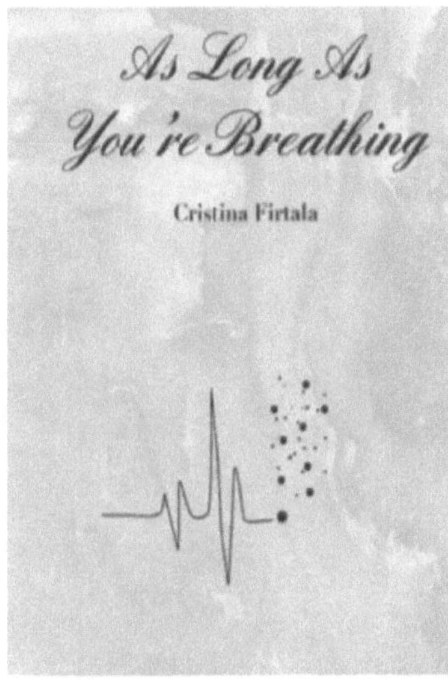

'As Long As You're Breathing' is a collection of poems
about, love, purpose and existence. Within each poem
exists a realisation, an awakening of the power and
worth we withhold, that there is always so much more
than our emotions and difficulties conceal. It brings to
life the parts of our existence we struggle with or cannot
confront, through hopeful messages, empowering
imagery and worded therapy that could be a salvation.
All of which guides the reader towards answering one
question... What do you do when the world consumes
you- from within?

You are, your cure.

You are, your cure.

The Perfect Loss

Cristina Firtala

We all know the story of sickness, the soul aching battle to heal. But what about the story where mental health falls in love with physical health, who survives that love story, or shall I say…who makes it out alive?

A short, but intense novel of the raw, brutal realities of suffering, loss and a love that comes at the ultimate expense of death, acceptance and reality.

Romeo and Snow, two opposite souls who share different versions of the same trauma. Initially Snow struggles with her mental health, overflowing with obstacles that she could never imagine, while Romeo fights a sickness, polished with the desire to live. A love story, or shall I say a love battle, between the desire to live, and the desire to just exist. When Snow finds out that things, people and the world is nothing like she imagined, the truth unveils and she is left alone, obligated to find her way out. To create her own exit, but things are not that simple, along the way she makes a terrible mistake, one that paralyzed her mind into the desire to find justice, to restore the balance. But will she forgive herself, or will she spiral down that path?

A story that exposes; grief for raw reality of what it is truly like, love for its undiscovered depths and trauma for the hidden, buried pieces that float to the shore of our minds.

What stage in life are you in?

Trapped?
Lost?
Exhausted?

You are, your cure.

Well, don't worry, each stage has an answer, and hopefully, this story will guide you to where you need to find it.

You are, your cure.